Babe, The Sheep-Pig

A play by David Wood

Adapted from the book *The Sheep-Pig* by Dick King-Smith

Samuel French — London
New York - Toronto - Hollywood

ISBN 0 573 05115 1

Please see page iv for further copyright information

BABE, THE SHEEP-PIG

First performed at the New Victoria Theatre, Woking on November 18th, 1997, as part of a tour, including a Christmas season at the Forum Theatre, Wythenshawe. The production, presented by Whirligig Theatre in association with Manchester Library Theatre and the Birmingham Hippodrome, was made possible by Barclays Stage Partnership, a sponsorship scheme from Barclays and the Arts Council of England. The cast, in alphabetical order, was as follows:

Gary Bates	**Puppy 1, Shepherd, Duck**
Karen Briffett	**Babe**
David Burrows	**TV Commentator, Vicar, Cockerel**
Emma Clayton	**Sheep 1, Cat, Duck**
Mary-Ann Coburn	**Fly**
Reece Cooper	**Duck**
Amanda Kernot	**Duck**
Kirsty Kinnear	**Ma, Sheep-dog, Turkey**
Anthony Pedley	**Farmer Hogget**
Judy Wilson	**Mrs Hogget**
Cliff Atkinson	Keyboards

Weight Guessers, Stallholders, New Owners, Rustlers, Worrier-dogs, Nightmare Animals and **Officials** played by members of the cast. **Sheep** and **Puppies** were played by children recruited locally at each theatre

Director	**David Wood**
Sets and Costumes Designer	**Susie Caulcutt**
Director of Movement	**Sheila Falconer**
Music Composer	**Peter Pontzen**
Lighting Designer	**Robert Ornbo**
Sound Designer	**Mike Furness**
Associate Director	**Ben Forster**

SYNOPSIS OF SCENES

ACT I

The Showground of the Grand Challenge Sheep-dog Trials
The Village Fair

Farmer Hogget's Farm	Stable interior (loose-box)
	Farmyard/Farmhouse exterior
	Stable interior (loose-box)
	Farmhouse interior
	Field
	Farmhouse interior
	Farmyard
	Field

ACT II

Farmer Hogget's Farm	Field
	Farmyard / Farmhouse exterior
	Farmhouse interior
	Farmyard
	Field
	Farmyard/Stable interior (loose-box)

The Showground of the Grand Challenge Sheep-dog Trials (including Farmhouse interior inset)

Photographs
The photographs in this Acting Edition are from the
original designs and model by Susie Caulcutt and are
reproduced by permission of the photographer, Robert
Workman.

Music
Optional incidental music, composed by Peter Pontzen
for the original production, is available from Samuel
French Ltd.

Cast of Characters with Suggested Doubling

The original production employed ten actors and ten children. Companies with more actors available need not use these doubling suggestions. It would, however, be difficult to perform the play with less than ten principal actors.

Actor 1	**TV Commentator, Vicar, Cockerel, New Owner, Rustler, Worrier-dog, Nightmare Dog**
Actor 2	**Shepherd, Weight Guesser, Puppy 1, Duck, Rustler, Worrier-dog, Nightmare Animal**
Actor 3	**Sheep-dog, Weight Guesser, Turkey, Ma, Nightmare Animal, Official**
Actor 4	**Official, Stallholder, Weight Guesser, New Owner, Rustler, Duck, Nightmare Animal**
Actor 5	**Official, Stallholder, Rustler, Duck, Nightmare Animal**
Actor 6	**Sheep 1, Stallholder, Cat, Duck, New Owner, Nightmare Animal**
Actor 7	**Farmer Hogget**
Actor 8	**Fly**
Actor 9	**Mrs Hogget**
Actor 10	**Babe**

Actor 3 (**Ma**) and Actor 6 (**Sheep 1**) were joined by seven children to make up the flock of **Sheep**. More might be possible. Actor 2 (**Puppy 1**) was joined by three children who played the other puppies. Extras, children and adults, could be employed in the Trials scenes and at the Village Fair.

The Village Fair

INTRODUCTION

Soon after Dick King-Smith's *The Sheep-Pig* was published in 1983 my wife and I read it to our daughters. We all loved it and I was convinced it would become a classic. The successful film version entitled *Babe* further popularised the story and now I am proud to have been entrusted with its translation from page to stage. My hope is that amateurs and professionals, adults and children, will get as much pleasure from acting out the story as I have from adapting the book and directing the first production. This took place in traditional proscenium theatres, but I much look forward to seeing productions in arena spaces or in the round, which would be ideal for the Sheep-dog Trials and the Village Fair.

Settings should not be too complex or unwieldy. A large open space is necessary for the Sheep-dog Trials and the scenes in the Field. Small "gates" or fence sections could be useful in creating obstacles and pens and also the edge of the Field and Farmyard. The Stable loose-box and the Farmhouse could be small, movable trucks.

I have tried to keep the play flowing, without having clearly defined scene endings with black-outs. Narration helps this, of course, but it does mean that the cast must sometimes become scene-shifters, changing the setting in vision. This makes me wonder if the cast (most of them, anyway) should wear a simple basic costume, to which is added a head, a coat or an extra layer to suggest the characters. I also like the notion that the cast are understood to be storytellers as well as characters. Rather than trying to be naturalistic, a virtue can be made out of the fact that human beings are playing animals, in an imaginative way.

This, of course, applies to the movement too. All the animals should be on two legs, not four, and a language needs to be found to make this both amusing and acceptable, so that the audience can enjoy and believe in the characters, especially when they are inter-relating with human beings. The more stylized movement envisaged for the training sequences, the Rustlers' scene, the sheep-worrying, the death of Ma and the Nightmare should not be too choreographed, but integrated into the general movement style.

For the final triumphant performance by Babe and the Sheep I have suggested that the Sheep move in rhythmic precision, to music, in a way that is different from the other sheep-training sequences; I want it to seem almost magical, amusing too, a fitting climax to the play. Hopefully this will get over the "problem" that the audience is bound to know all will end successfully. If the situation lacks the tension of uncertainty, it could gain from witty execution.

Incidentally, the map of the Sheep-dog Trials course, to be found in the original book version of *The Sheep-Pig*, is a very useful guide.

Finally my thanks to Dick King-Smith for writing a splendidly theatrical story and for generously approving this adaptation.

David Wood

Farmer Hogget's Farmhouse

For the Whirligig team, back on the road
with this play—my thanks for all your
support, skill and stamina over the years.

D.W.

OTHER PLAYS AND MUSICALS BY DAVID WOOD

Aladdin
The BFG (based on the book by Roald Dahl)
Babes in the Magic Wood
Cinderella
Dick Whittington and Wondercat
Dinosaurs and all that Rubbish (based on the book by Michael Foreman)
Flibberty and the Penguin
The Gingerbread Man
Hijack Over Hygenia
The Ideal Gnome Expedition
Jack and the Giant
Jack the Lad (co-written with Dave and Toni Arthur)
Larry the Lamb in Toytown (co-written with Sheila Ruskin, adapted from
the stories of S.G. Hulme-Beaman)
Meg and Mog Show (from the books by Helen Nicoll and Jan
Pieńkowski)
More Adventures of Noddy (based on the stories by Enid Blyton)
Mother Goose's Golden Christmas
Noddy (based on the stories by Enid Blyton)
Nutcracker Sweet
Old Father Time
The Old Man of Lochnagar (based on the book by HRH The Prince of
Wales)
Old Mother Hubbard
The Owl and the Pussycat Went to See... (co-written with Sheila Ruskin)
The Papertown Paperchase
The Pied Piper (co-written with Dave and Toni Arthur)
The Plotters of Cabbage Patch Corner
Robin Hood (co-written with Dave and Toni Arthur)
Rupert and the Green Dragon (based on the *Rupert* stories and characters
by Mary Tourtel and Alfred Bestall)
Save the Human (based on the story by Tony Husband and David Wood)
The See-Saw Tree
The Selfish Shellfish
There Was An Old Woman...
Tickle (one act)
The Witches (based on the book by Roald Dahl)

Theatre for Children—Guide to Writing, Adapting, Directing and Acting
(written with Janet Grant, published by Faber and Faber)

ACT I

After a short overture, which might sound like a television introductory theme, we hear distant thunder and the sound of rain and wind

A Light finds a television commentator with a microphone. He carries an umbrella

TV Commentator Welcome viewers, to the exciting closing stages of the Grand Challenge Sheep-dog Trials.

General Lighting increases to reveal a field and a cloudy sky. Perhaps a banner proclaims "Grand Challenge Sheep-dog Trials"

A group of Sheep huddle restlessly upstage as a Shepherd and his dog stand downstage. The Shepherd blows a whistle

As you join us, Mr Jones from Wales and his dog, Bryn, are starting their round.

The dog circles the field and begins to chivvy the Sheep forward towards the first obstacle. As the round progresses, the Sheep do not co-operate very well, occasionally scattering, with the odd Sheep breaking away from the group. The Shepherd occasionally blows his whistle and shouts instructions— "steady", "stay", "down", "away to me" or "come by". Perhaps there is occasional applause from the crowd

Down from the Holding Post ... the sheep aren't too keen ... hardly blame them in this weather ... through the Fetch Gates ... one gone the wrong way, points lost for that ... round the Handler's Post and away ... looking a little ragged ... through the Drive Away Gates, nicely through, big crowd here today, they enjoyed that ... towards the Cross Drive Gates ... a mistake there, go on Bryn, get them back ... good recovery ... into the Shedding ring, nicely, nicely ... now the trickiest bit, shedding the sheep with collars...

The dog tries to separate the Sheep, who resist. They bunch and revolve

…that's a shame, he's lost points there … and finally, into the pen … yes, yes! Good effort, Bryn… Mr Jones will be happy with that.

Applause from the crowd. The Shepherd blows his whistle. The dog returns to him

Shepherd That'll do!
TV Commentator Here comes the score…

An official holds up two cards with an eight and a five

Dog and Shepherd exit and an official ushers the Sheep off stage

Eighty-five! Puts them in the lead. A good score considering the appalling weather conditions. It's difficult to see that score being beaten, but here comes the last competitor to try to do just that.

7:00

Farmer Hogget, carrying his crook, and Fly enter and stand C

It's Farmer Hogget with Pig. A bit of a strange name that. And a surprise. Usually Farmer Hogget works with a dog called Fly … in fact, I think that *is* Fly.

Suddenly Farmer Hogget sends Fly to one side   to 7:00

Hallo, what's happening?

Fly ushers on Babe, who goes to Farmer Hogget

Good heavens! I don't believe it! It *is* a pig!

After a stunned moment of silence, the sound of laughter from the crowd builds and builds as the sound of rain and wind recedes. Babe looks apprehensive yet almost defiant. Farmer Hogget stands motionless

The Commentator, laughing, exits

Suddenly, at its peak, the laughter cuts out as the Lighting changes, focusing on Babe, Farmer Hogget, and Fly, who breaks downstage   Circle + present Babe

Fly (*to the audience*) That's my son. (*She looks at Babe, then back to the audience*) Well, my adopted son. And this is the most important day in his life. In Farmer Hogget's life too.
Farmer Hogget Steady, Pig.

Fly He's my boss. Why, you may be wondering, has he entered a pig in the Grand Challenge Sheep-dog Trials?

Other members of the cast enter and stand facing the audience as the Lighting increases a little

(*Taking in the other members of the cast*) We'll tell you. We'll tell you the story of...

All Babe, the Sheep-Pig!

Music as the cast swiftly change the scene. The banner disappears. The obstacles (fences or straw bales) are used to create homespun fairground stalls like ball-in-a-bucket, an Aunt Sally (stallholder poking his head through a hole in a funny picture and having children throw "wet" sponges at him), a bran tub, a simple hoopla, a home produce stall, and a stall with a sign saying "Guess My Weight", run by the Vicar. Perhaps his church is visible. The music might sound homespun too. Perhaps a small group of children play or sing throughout the scene. But we must be able to hear the dialogue

EXIT

11:00

Fly (*to the audience*) It all started at the village fair.

Music continues as the village fair comes to life

Children visit the stalls

Stallholders Roll up, roll up!
  Ball-in-a-bucket. Three throws for ten p!
  Prize every time!
  Hoopla! Hoopla! One ring over one bottle to win!
  Bran tub! Bran tub! (*Etc. etc.*)

At regular intervals a high-pitched squeal is heard from the "Guess My Weight" stall, but we can't see what is happening because of the small crowd gathered round

The Vicar, holding a clipboard, makes notes

Once the scene is established, Farmer Hogget enters, carrying a basket of goodies covered with a cloth. He looks about for the home produce stall, sees it, and delivers the basket

Stallholder Afternoon, Farmer Hogget. Oh, thank you! These look lovely. (*She starts displaying them on the stall*)

The squealing is heard again

Farmer Hogget walks away from the stall. Suddenly a phone rings. At first Farmer Hogget doesn't react, but then he stops and pulls out a mobile phone from his pocket. He is clearly unfamiliar with its working. He puts it to his ear

Farmer Hogget Hallo?

The phone keeps ringing. Farmer Hogget looks at it, shakes it, then shakes his head. A child nearby approaches, understands the problem, takes the phone, pulls out its aerial and presses a button. The ringing stops. The child hands back the phone

(*Nodding appreciatively*) Mmm. Darn thing. Free gift with the new Land Rover.

The child smiles and wanders off

(*Into the phone*) Hallo?

Mrs Hogget enters downstage in a separate pool of light. She talks into an ordinary phone

Mrs Hogget Is that you?
Farmer Hogget Who?
Mrs Hogget You. Hogget, is that you?
Farmer Hogget Aah.

Another squeal

Mrs Hogget Are you there?
Farmer Hogget Where?
Mrs Hogget At the fair.
Farmer Hogget Aah.
Mrs Hogget Have you delivered my cakes and jams and pickles and preserves?
Farmer Hogget Aah.

Another squeal

Mrs Hogget What's that noise?
Farmer Hogget What noise?

Another squeal, longer and louder

Mrs Hogget *That* noise.

Farmer Hogget wanders over to the "Guess My Weight" stall. As he arrives, the crowd clears enough for us to see a pig—Babe—being held up over a pen or straw bale. Eventually Weight Guesser 1 lowers the pig out of sight, and the squealing stops

Farmer Hogget Pig.
Weight Guesser 1 Twenty-eight pounds.
Vicar (*writing on his clipboard*) Thank you, Mrs Williams.
Mrs Hogget Pig? I thought 'twas a pig, I said to meself that's a pig that is, only nobody round here do keep pigs, 'tis all sheep for miles about.

Weight Guesser 2 pays his money and lifts the pig

More squealing. Mrs Hogget reacts to the noise

What's it doing? Anybody'd think they was killing the poor thing.

Weight Guesser 2 puts the pig down. The squealing stops

Weight Guesser 2 Thirty-three pounds.
Vicar Thank you, sir.
Farmer Hogget Got to guess its weight. Nearest guess wins.
Mrs Hogget What?
Farmer Hogget What?
Mrs Hogget Wins what?
Farmer Hogget Pig.
Vicar Afternoon, Farmer Hogget. Fancy a go?
Farmer Hogget (*to the Vicar*) Well…
Mrs Hogget What?
Farmer Hogget Vicar wants me to have a go.
Mrs Hogget Go on then. I'd like a pig. We could feed 'un on scraps, he'd come just right for Christmas time, just think, two nice hams, two sides of bacon, pork chops, kidney, liver, chitterling, trotters, save his blood for black pudding, lovely, you have a go.
Farmer Hogget Aah. (*He manages to turn off the mobile phone and puts it in his pocket*)

Mrs Hogget exits

Music as Farmer Hogget approaches the stall and gives the Vicar a coin

Vicar Thank you, Farmer Hogget. (*He indicates the pig*) Try your luck.

Farmer Hogget reaches over and gently but firmly lifts the pig. They look at each other. The pig doesn't squeal

Music and possibly Lighting heighten the significance of the moment. People turn to look. All the other fair activity stops. A frozen tingly moment

(*Quietly*) Extraordinary. For everyone else he screams his head off. He seems to like you, Farmer Hogget.

We can tell that Farmer Hogget is thinking "I like him, too" but he doesn't say it

After a pause…

Farmer Hogget Thirty-one pounds. And a quarter.

The Lighting focuses down on Farmer Hogget and Babe, still staring at each other

The scene around them begins to clear in the half-light as Fly returns to narrate

Music continues to echo the almost magical "connection" between Farmer Hogget and Babe

12:00

Fly The boss must have guessed right. Because that evening we had a new arrival on the farm.

Music as Farmer Hogget and Babe break their freeze. Farmer Hogget either carries or accompanies Babe to a stable loose-box made of straw bales. The Lighting suggests early evening

Farmer Hogget gently lays Babe down, then exits

Babe nervously takes in his new surroundings

Suddenly Fly's four Puppies enter and, curious, look over the side of the straw bales

Puppy 1 What's that?
Puppy 2 It's funny!

Puppy 3 It's ugly!
Puppy 4 It's horrible!

The Puppies laugh unkindly

Puppy 1 (*calling*) Hey, Mum, look at this!

Fly joins them. She sees Babe

What is it?
Fly It's a pig.
Puppy 1 What will the boss do with it?
Fly Eat it. When it's big enough.
Puppy 2 Will he eat us?
Puppy 3 When we're big enough?
Fly Bless you, people only eat stupid animals. Like sheep and cows and ducks and chickens. They don't eat clever ones like dogs.
Puppy 4 So pigs are stupid?
Fly (*after a thinking pause*) Yes. Pigs are stupid.

Babe looks up at her

Puppy 1 It certainly *looks* stupid.
Puppies (*chanting*) Stupid, stupid, stupid, stupid!

Fly hushes them

Fly (*to Babe*) Hallo. Who are you?
Babe (*with an effort*) I'm a Large White.
Puppy 1 Blimey! If that's a large white, what's a small one like?

The Puppies roar with laughter

Fly Be quiet! Just remember that five minutes ago you didn't even know what a pig was. (*To Babe*) I expect Large White's your breed, dear. I meant what's your name?
Babe I don't know.
Fly Well, what did your mother call you, to tell you apart from your brothers and sisters?

The memory of his siblings and his mother affects Babe

Babe (*voice trembling*) She called us all the same.

Fly And what was that, dear?
Babe Babe.

The Puppies giggle unkindly

Fly (*to the Puppies*) Hush. (*To Babe*) But that's a lovely name. Would you like us to call you that? It'll make you feel more at home.

The memory of home affects Babe

Babe I want my mum.

After a brief pause, the Puppies laugh again

Puppy 1 Aaaah! He wants his mum!
Puppies (*chanting*) Mum, mum, mum, mum!
Fly Stop it. Go out into the yard and play.
Puppies Ohhhhh!
Fly Go on. Shoo!

The Puppies exit

Fly climbs over and joins Babe, who at first reacts nervously

Listen, Babe, you've got to be a brave boy. Everyone has to leave their mother, it's all part of growing up. I did so, when I was your age, and my puppies will have to leave me quite soon. But I'll look after you. If you like. (*She looks at Babe welcomingly*)

Pause. Then music as Babe cuddles up to her

Suddenly Farmer Hogget and Mrs Hogget enter and make their way towards the loose-box. Farmer Hogget carries a water-bowl

Mrs Hogget Well, what a turn-up. Never won nothing before, have you Hogget? Not a sausage let alone a whole pig!

They arrive and look into the loose-box

Well, will you look at that! That old Fly, she'll mother anything, kittens, ducklings, baby chicks, she's looked after all of they, now 'tis a pig, in't he lovely, what a picture, good job he don't know where he'll finish up, but he'll be big then and we'll be glad to see the back of him, or the hams of him, I should say, shan't us?

Farmer Hogget puts down the water-bowl and gives Babe a friendly stroke

Farmer Hogget Pity, really.

They start to leave

Mrs Hogget (*with a laugh*) Wonder how I shall get him all in the freezer!

Farmer Hogget and Mrs Hogget exit

Music. The Lighting fades a little more. It is night

The Puppies return and climb into the loose-box

Puppy 1 Oh, Mum! What's that stupid Babe doing here?
Puppy 2 Tell him to move over.
Puppy 3 He'll wet the bed.
Puppies Ughhhhh!
Fly Hush. Don't be so rude. (*To Babe*) If you want to do anything, dear, you
go outside, there's a good boy.
Puppy 4 (*threatening*) Yeah, you'd better.

All settle down

Fly Night, puppies.
Puppies Night, Mum.
Fly Night, Babe.
Babe (*after a pause*) Night, Mum.

Music and Lighting suggest the passage of time, from night through to dawn

Cockerel enters, struts about for a while, then takes up a position of importance

Cockerel Cock-a-doodle-dooooo!

Music as Fly, the Puppies and Babe stir and stretch

Farmer Hogget enters. He goes to the loose-box and "opens" it

Farmer Hogget Morning. Fly, come sit.

*Fly steps forward and sits. She nods to Puppy 1, who joins her and sits. Then
Puppy 2. Then Puppy 3. Then Puppy 4*

Pause. Then Babe, unprompted, comes forward and sits too. All—dogs and the farmer—look at him, surprised

Fly, out!   9:00

Fly goes "out" and waits. She nods to Puppy 1, who follows. Then Puppy 2. Then Puppy 3. Then Puppy 4

Pause. Then Babe, unprompted, starts to follow

Not you, Pig.

Babe looks appealingly up at him

Go on then!

Babe joins the others

Fly Come on, Babe. We'll show you round the farmyard.

Music as Fly leads the procession of Puppies and Babe round the farmyard. As Farmer Hogget clears away the loose-box, the exterior of the farmhouse appears the other side

Once the scene is set, Farmer Hogget exits

The procession passes by Cockerel. All nod to each other. Cockerel does a double take when he sees Babe

Cockerel What-the-doodle? Who are you?
Fly (*returning*) Babe, this is Cockerel. Cockerel, Babe.
Cockerel (*disdainfully*) Babe? How-do-doodle-doo.
Babe I'm a pig.
Cockerel Yes. Cock-a-doodle-pooooooo!

Babe looks affronted, but thinks better of replying

Fly Come on, dear. Take no notice.

Cockerel exits as the procession continues

Cat enters

Look, it's Cat. Let's have some fun.

Fly playfully leaps at Cat, making her recoil. Puppy 1 imitates Fly. Cat recoils. Puppies 2, 3 and 4 all do the same. Cat recoils, but doesn't retaliate

Babe now has a go. This time Cat springs and wields a sharp claw. Babe recoils

Babe Sorry!
Fly Don't worry, dear. Move faster next time.

As Cat exits, Turkey enters

Babe Who's that?
Fly Turkey.

Babe approaches. Turkey struts menacingly

Not too close!
Babe (*politely*) Good morning, Turkey.

Turkey looks at him

What do *you* do?
Turkey (*haughtily*) I gobble and I peck. (*He stares at Babe*)
Babe Oh. Thank you. (*He turns to leave*)

Turkey lunges and pecks him

Ow!

Turkey exits majestically

(*Returning to Fly*) They're not very friendly.
Fly You'll learn, dear. Do as I do and you'll be fine.

Music as Mrs Hogget enters from the farmhouse and Farmer Hogget enters from the other side

Mrs Hogget puts down a bowl of slops for Babe. Farmer Hogget puts down a trough of dog food

Ah, breakfast!

Fly and the Puppies go and tuck into their food

Mrs Hogget (*calling*) Come, Pig, snuffle up your slops! Got to get you nice
   and chubby!

*Babe approaches, sniffs the slops, then deliberately goes over to Fly and the
Puppies and squeezes his way in to share the dog food. Farmer Hogget and
Mrs Hogget look at each other in surprise, then at the dogs and the pig
polishing off the food*

   When they have finished Farmer Hogget takes off the trough

   Mrs Hogget takes the bowl of slops into the house

Babe, interested, follows her

Fly Not in the farmhouse, dear.
Babe Aren't pigs allowed in there?
Puppy 1 (*under his breath*) Not live ones.

The other Puppies snigger

Fly No dear, not yet anyway.
Puppy 1 You wait.
Babe Wait for what?

The Puppies snigger. Fly gives the Puppies a severe look

Fly Er——

   Farmer Hogget returns

Farmer Hogget Come, Fly.
Fly —you wait here with the boys, Babe, while I see to the sheep. I shan't
   be long.

   Fly exits with Farmer Hogget

Babe What's sheep?
Puppy 1 Don't you know that, you silly Babe? Sheep are animals.
Puppy 2 With thick woolly coats.
Puppy 3 And thick woolly heads.
Puppy 4 They're thick.
Puppies Thick, thick!
Puppy 1 And men can't look after them without the help of the likes of us.

Babe Why do they need you?
Puppies Because we're sheep-dogs!

They all roar with laughter, then start a friendly chasing game, in which Babe happily joins in. All end up rolling in a heap, laughing

> *As they settle down, the Lighting changes, picking up Fly, who enters watching the Puppies and Babe playing*

Fly (*to the audience*) After a few weeks, Babe became just like one of my puppies. And after a few more weeks came the day I was dreading…

Music as she joins Babe and the Puppies

> *Farmer Hogget brings on a couple of straw bales and places them behind the animals, as Mrs Hogget brings New Owner 1 from the farmhouse*

Babe distances himself a little from the dogs

The following scene is mimed as clearly as possible, avoiding too much sentimentality

Farmer Hogget greets New Owner 1, who hands over some money. He is invited to view the Puppies, who look up, not fully understanding

New Owner 1 chooses a puppy. Farmer Hogget singles him out, but before he can hand him over, Fly and the puppy say their goodbyes

> *New Owner 1 exits, taking the puppy, as New Owner 2 is brought in by Mrs Hogget*

The action is repeated. Money changes hands. New Owner 2 chooses two puppies. Fly and the puppies say goodbye

> *New Owner 2 and puppies leave*

> *New Owner 3 enters*

Same action

> *After Fly says goodbye, the final puppy is led away*

Fly is left empty and alone. After a pause, Babe approaches gently

Babe You've still got me. (*Meaningfully*) Mum.

Fly (*bravely*) I've still got you. (*Without looking at him*) For a while. (*With a genuine smile*) That's nice.

Babe Mum.

Fly Yes, dear?

Babe They've gone off to work sheep, haven't they?

Fly Yes, dear.

Babe Because they're sheep-dogs. Like you. You're useful to the boss, aren't you, because you're a sheep-dog.

Fly Yes, dear.

Babe Mum.

Fly Yes, dear?

Babe Why can't I learn to be a sheep-*pig*?

Fly (*to the audience*) A sheep-pig! No chance! But to humour him I tried to teach Babe to be a duck-pig!

Suddenly the Lighting brightens and the music changes as four quacking Ducks waddle in

In a comic, choreographed sequence, Fly shouts instructions to Babe, who tries to manoeuvre the Ducks through the straw bales

(*To Babe*) Drive them through here, Babe. Away to me. No. This way.

Babe chases the Ducks, who refuse to co-operate. Whatever Babe does, they never go through the gap, veering wildly to one side or the other, quacking crossly. Eventually...

Babe It's no good, Mum. I tell them what to do, but they won't listen.

Fly Show them you mean business. Watch.

Babe watches and sees a completely new side of Fly, who stalks the Ducks, who twist and turn in fright. Suddenly Fly dashes at them

Go on, you daft ducks! Move!

The Ducks waddle through the gap and exit

Fly returns to Babe

See? You'll learn. Remember, they're stupid, just like sheep. And dogs are intelligent.

Babe But I'm a pig.

Fly (*realizing she is eating her former words*) Pigs are intelligent too.
Babe Mum, do you suppose, if I were to ask them politely…
Fly Ask them politely? What an idea! (*She laughs uproariously*)

Babe wanders off thoughtfully

There is a sudden clap of thunder, to which Fly reacts. Then rain. The Lighting fades down as Farmer Hogget clears away the straw bales and the stable loose-box is set

exit 12.00

Fly exits as, in the shadows, we are aware that Farmer Hogget is tending an animal. This is Ma, a sheep. After a short while Farmer Hogget leaves

Lights up as the rain continues softly and Ma coughs, a rasping sickly cough

Babe appears and curiously approaches the loose-box, but he can't see Ma

Babe Hallo?

Ma coughs again

(*Louder*) Hallo?
Ma Go away, wolf. Nag, nag, nag all day long, go here, go there, do this, do that. Go away, wolf. Give us a bit of peace.
Babe I'm not a wolf.
Ma Oh, I know all that. Call yourself a sheep-dog, I know that, but you don't fool none of us. You're a wolf, given half a chance. You looks at us and you sees lamb-chops.
Babe But I'm not a sheep-dog either. (*He looks over the side*) Look.
Ma Well, I'll be dipped. No more you ain't. What are you?
Babe Pig. What are you?
Ma Ewe.
Babe Not me. You.
Ma Ewe, that's right.

Babe looks confused

Sort of sheep.
Babe (*excited*) Sheep? I've never met a sheep before.
Ma Well, you has now. (*She coughs*) One sick sheep. Foot-rot. Cough. And I'm not as young as I was.

Babe climbs over to join Ma

Babe You don't look very old to me.

Ma Very civil of you to say so. First kind word I've heard since I were a little lamb.

Babe My name's Babe. What's yours?

Ma Maaaaa.

Suddenly Fly looks over the loose-box Enter 12:00

Fly (*sharply*) Babe, what are you doing?

Ma (*alarmed*) Wolf! Wolf!

~~**Babe** Talking to Ma.~~

Fly Huh! Save your breath, dear. (*Rudely to Ma*) Silly old fool. (*To Babe*) Waste of time talking to her. Come away.

Fly exits 7:00

Babe nearly goes, but hesitates

Ma Rude, rude, rude.

Babe She's kind really.

Ma No respect. No respect. At least she's not a worrier.

Babe What's a worrier?

Ma Sort of wolf as chases us, nips and bites. Even kills.

Babe Fly's not like that.

Ma No, just rude.

Fly (*off*) Babe! Here!

Babe I must go. (*Sudden idea*) Ma, when you're better, can I come and visit you in your field?

Ma I'd like that, young 'un. I'd like that. (*She has another coughing fit*)

Babe slips away

A clap of thunder. Ma reacts, then settles to sleep as the Lighting fades

In a setting light the loose-box disappears and the farmhouse interior is revealed

Meanwhile Fly returns to narrate C

Fly (*to the audience*) When Ma was better, the boss took her back to join the other sheep. One night they were safe in their pen and…

She crosses to the farmhouse as the Lights reveal Farmer Hogget and Mrs Hogget watching television

uc

…I was with the boss, watching television. (*She joins Farmer Hogget*)

The television programme is football or another sport. Perhaps Mrs Hogget is kneading dough

Mrs Hogget For the life of me, Hogget, I can't see why you do let that pig run all over the place like you do chasing my ducks about, shoving his nose into everything. Are you listening?

Farmer Hogget Aah. (*But he keeps watching the television*)

Mrs Hogget He's running all his flesh off, he won't never be fit for Christmas, Easter more like. What d'you call him?

Farmer Hogget Just Pig. (*He falls asleep during the following*)

Mrs Hogget Huh! More like a dog than a pig. Surprised as how you hasn't invited 'im in to watch the telly. Eh?

Farmer Hogget snores loudly. Mrs Hogget raises her eyebrows and attacks the dough

Music as the Light fades on the farmhouse

Through the half-light Babe makes his cautious yet determined way towards the field. He travels across and round until he arrives. The Sheep are all huddled downstage, perhaps in a pen (or this can be imagined). Babe gingerly approaches

Babe Excuse me.

The Sheep become restless

Sheep Wolf! Wolf! Baaa!

Babe No, no. I'm not a wolf. Please, I'm looking for Ma.

Sheep Maaaa, Maaaa.

Ma shuffles through the others

Ma Who's there?

Babe Hallo, Ma. It's me!

Ma Oh, it's you, young 'un. (*To the Sheep*) Settle down. 'Tis my friend, Babe!

Sheep Baaaabe, Baaaabe!

Ma Should you be out on your own in the dark?

Babe I wanted to see you.

Ma Very kind, I'm sure, but…

Suddenly they are interrupted by the loud, menacing rumble of a lorry approaching

Babe What's that?
Ma (*urgently*) Hush!

A screech of brakes. Through the gloom we see the back of the lorry silhouetted against the sky. The engine is running

Loud, echoing noises of doors opening and slamming. Music underscores the tension

Then four figures emerge with powerful torches, which probe the area and eventually find the Sheep

Babe creeps back, out of sight

Voices There they are! Come on! Hurry!

Two men slowly wind down the tailboard of the lorry, forming a ramp. Loud, echoing chain-rattling sounds. A clunking thud as the tailboard hits the ground

Babe creeps back to Ma

Babe What's happening?
Ma Rustlers. They'm sheep rustlers, Babe. Sheep-stealers. We'll all be in that lorry afore you can blink your eye.

The Sheep, realizing the danger, start to jostle and panic

Sheep Baaa! Baaa!
Ma Go, Babe, run for it, quick!
Babe But...

Suddenly the Rustlers approach, wielding large sticks. Babe retreats as they unpen the Sheep and start driving them towards the lorry

Rustlers (*savagely*) Move! Move!

The Sheep try to stick together, heading across rather than up. The Rustlers race round to outflank them

Go on! Move!

The Sheep are forced toward the lorry. The Rustlers threaten with their sticks

Suddenly, Babe runs round the Sheep and the Rustlers and up the ramp. He turns

Babe Please! I beg you. Sheep, dear sensible sheep…

A rustle of approval runs throughout the Sheep

…stop! Don't come any further.

The Sheep stop. The Rustlers stop in surprise

Please! Turn round!

The Sheep turn, jostling the Rustlers

Run! Run!

The Sheep rush through the Rustlers, scatter in all directions, then exit

The Rustlers recover themselves

Rustlers Get him! Get him!

They charge at Babe, sticks aloft. But when they go to strike, the sticks crash against each other, and from underneath Babe escapes and watches as the Rustlers lash out and hit each other. Perhaps this develops into a short slapstick episode ending with the Rustlers all unconscious

A musical chord of triumph. Then Babe squeals. A piercing squeal of warning. It echoes nightmarishly as the Lighting fades and the scene changes

Lights up on the farmhouse

The Hoggets and Fly are as we last saw them

The squealing continues. Farmer Hogget wakes up as Fly jumps up

Fly Babe!
Mrs Hogget It's the pig!

Farmer Hogget grabs the phone and dials 999

Immediately a police car siren blares out, taking over from the squealing

Black-out apart from a revolving blue light to suggest a police car lamp

After a while, the siren fades and the Lights come up on the farmyard, where Fly addresses us and Cockerel, Turkey, Cat and the Ducks

Fly The Rustlers were caught. The sheep were saved. And it's all thanks to…
All Babe!

Music strikes up as Babe appears

The other animals dance a celebratory dance around him. Each musical phrase is punctuated by the shout of "Babe"

After a final, triumphant flourish, the animals freeze. Fly and Babe are together

Farmer Hogget and Mrs Hogget enter through the assembly of animals

Mrs Hogget And if you think we're going to eat him after what he's done, you've got another think coming, Hogget. He's saved our bacon, so we'll save *his*!

The animals, unseen by the Hoggets, cheer ecstatically. Farmer Hogget, for the first time, smiles broadly

The animals exit happily

Mrs Hogget exits too

Farmer Hogget, Fly and Babe remain

Farmer Hogget Come, Fly. Collect the sheep.

Fly joins him. They turn to go. Babe watches. Suddenly Farmer Hogget turns

Come, Pig.

Babe, delighted, follows. All three, to music, set off to the field   5,00

They circle the stage as the Sheep enter in a huddle upstage in one corner of the field

Farmer Hogget , Fly and Babe arrive in the opposite diagonal corner

7:00

Babe What's happening, Mum?
Fly The boss wants me to bring the sheep down to him. You stay and watch.
Farmer Hogget (*blowing his whistle*) Come by!

Fly runs to the Sheep. They all turn their backs on her

Sheep Wolf! Wolf!
Fly (*threateningly*) Move, fools. Down the hill. If you know which way
"down" is.

The Sheep, in mutinous fashion, turn towards Fly

Sheep (*in chorus*)　　No, no, no
　　　　　　　　　　　　We's had enough
　　　　　　　　　　　　You've no ma-a-a-a-nners
　　　　　　　　　　　　Treat us rough
　　　　　　　　　　　　We's not stupid
　　　　　　　　　　　　We's quite bright
　　　　　　　　　　　　We'll obey if you
　　　　　　　　　　　　Treat us right.
　　　　　　　　　　　　Ba-a-a-a-a!

Fly lurches angrily towards the Sheep. But they won't be moved

Ma We want Babe!

The Sheep join in and chant

Sheep　　　　　　　　We want Babe!
　　　　　　　　　　　　We want Babe!
　　　　　　　　　　　　We want Ba-a-a-a-be!

*Music for tension, strange, almost magical, like when Farmer Hogget first
picked up Babe at the village fair*

Fly retreats, beaten

*Slowly Babe steps forward to meet her. Both turn to Farmer Hogget, who is
scratching his head, bemused*

Farmer Hogget (*almost in a trance*) Stay, Fly.

Fly returns to him

Come by, Pig!

Babe trots toward the Sheep. Music holds the tension. Babe stops

Babe Good morning. I do hope I find you all well and not too distressed by
yesterday's experience.

Sheep   Bless his heart
                             He's so polite
                             He knows how to
                             Treat us right!
                             Ba-a-a-a-a!

Babe Please, I want to be a sheep-pig. So. If I might ask a great favour of you.
Could you all be kind enough to walk down to my boss, the farmer? Take
your time, please, there's absolutely no rush.

Sheep   Oh what ma-a-a-a-anners
                             He's a treasure!
                             Yes, yes, yes
                             'Twould be our pleasure.
                             Ba-a-a-a-a!

*Without fuss, the Sheep progress in an orderly fashion down to Farmer
Hogget, who stands amazed*

Fly goes round to meet Babe

Fly Beautifully done, dear. The fools wouldn't do it for me.
Babe But they're *not* fools, Mum. If you ask them nicely…
Fly Hey, look.

Farmer Hogget is indicating Ma with his crook. He blows his whistle

The boss wants that old ewe shedded.
Babe Ma? What's shedded?
Fly Separated from the others. He wants to check her over.
Babe I'll do it.
Fly (*laughing*) Bet you won't, Babe. She hates being shedded, that one.

Babe goes over to the Sheep

Babe Hallo, again.

The Sheep turn towards him

Sheep A-a-a-a-ah! Ba-a-a-abe!

Babe Thank you for coming down so nicely. (*He calls*) Ma!

Ma Yes, young 'un?

Babe Would you mind coming over here? The boss wants to see if your foot-rot's better.

Ma Oh, not again. All that prodding…

Babe He's only trying to help, Ma. Come along, please.

Ma Oh, all right then, young 'un. Anything to oblige you. (*She emerges from the other Sheep*)

Farmer Hogget and Fly look on, amazed. Farmer Hogget comes forward and examines Ma's foot

(*Over Farmer Hogget's head*) Tell you what, young 'un. You'll make a wunnerful sheep-pig, or my name's not Ma-a-a-a-a!

The Sheep join in the praise. Their bleats echo like hoorays to end the scene

Sheep Ba-a-a-a-a! Ba-a-a-a-a! Ba-a-a-a-a-a-a-a!

Farmer Hogget, satisfied with Ma's foot, stands. Ma returns to the other Sheep

Farmer Hogget nods gratefully to Babe, then exits

Babe wanders happily off as Fly comes forward to narrate

The Sheep wander c as she talks

Fly (*to the audience*) From that day on, Babe helped with the sheep every day. The boss used him more and more.

Babe (*calling*) Are you sure you don't mind, Mum?

Fly Of course not. Less work for me to do. (*To the audience*) Sometimes, after work, Babe would visit the sheep, though why he wanted to be friends with them I never understood. All was fine.

Babe joins the Sheep

Until one day…

Fly exits *1 . 00*

Suddenly the atmosphere changes. Menacing music. The Lighting dims

Two Worrier-dogs enter, slowly edging towards the Sheep

The slow-motion is accentuated in a stylised, choreographed sequence during which the dogs attack the Sheep. They chase them. The Sheep react terrified

Perhaps distorted bleating and barking accompanies the discordant music

Babe watches aghast, then tries to fight off the dogs, who attack him

In the confusion only Ma is unable to move fast enough to escape serious mauling. She is too old and weak to resist

As the other Sheep look on, helpless, the dogs attack Ma and bring her to the ground

In stylised slow-motion they bite ferociously. Babe tries to help Ma

He manages to fight off the dogs, who make their escape

The Sheep slowly and formally form a semi-circle round Ma, as Babe tries unsuccessfully to revive her. He shakes his head in despair. She is dead

Suddenly Farmer Hogget, carrying a double-barrelled shotgun, and Fly enter. They survey the scene

Babe looks up in anguish. But Farmer Hogget, thinking Babe has savaged Ma, has no alternative. As Fly watches disbelievingly, he lifts the shotgun, cocks it, and aims it at Babe's head

Black-out

ACT II

The CURTAIN *rises on the field. The action at the end of Act I is reprised*

Babe looks crestfallen at the dying Ma, surrounded by the Sheep in a semi-circle

Farmer Hogget and Fly enter

After surmising the situation, Farmer Hogget cocks his shotgun and raises it towards Babe's head

As he is about to pull the trigger, we suddenly hear the ringing of a phone. Farmer Hogget hesitates, lowers the gun and takes out his mobile phone

Farmer Hogget Hallo?

Mrs Hogget enters in a separate pool of light. She talks animatedly into a phone

Mrs Hogget Hogget, be that you?
Farmer Hogget Aah.
Mrs Hogget What dost think then, the police have been on, they're ringing every farmer in the district to warn 'em, there's sheep-worrying dogs about, they killed six sheep t'other side of the valley only last night.

Pause. Farmer Hogget looks again at Ma, and then at Babe

Hogget, you there?
Farmer Hogget Aah.
Mrs Hogget Watch out for sheep-worriers, you hear?
Farmer Hogget I hear. (*He turns the phone off*)

Mrs Hogget exits

Farmer Hogget looks at Babe

Sheep-worriers eh? (*With a smile*) I reckon you gave them summat to worry about. Eh? Good Pig.

He breaks the shotgun, removes the cartridges and exits

Fly looks on, proudly

The Sheep chant in praise of the heroic Babe

Sheep Ba-a-a-a-a-abe! Ba-a-a-a-a-abe! BA-A-A-A-ABE!

But Babe doesn't respond. He sadly looks down at Ma

Babe Oh, Ma.

Music as the Sheep "sing" a lament to Ma—a simple, sad bleat of tribute

> *During their lament, Farmer Hogget returns and gently lifts the dead Ma and carries her off, followed respectfully by Fly and Babe, and, like choirboys, all the Sheep*

Sheep   M-a-a-a-a-a
                              M-a-a-a-a-a
                              M-a-a-a-a-a
                              M-a-a-a-a-a
                              M-a-a-a-a-a
                              M-a-a-a-a-a
                              M-a-a-a-a-a-a-a-a.

As the procession exits, the Lights slowly fade to black   Out 11:00

The scene changes to the farmhouse

Meanwhile, Fly enters downstage to narrate   11:00 to C

Fly Ma was dead. But somehow the boss knew that Babe had tried to save her. He told Mrs Hogget and she was so proud of him she started calling him to the back door…

Mrs Hogget enters

Mrs Hogget *(calling)* Pig! Here, Pig!

Babe enters and goes to her

Fly …and offering him juicy titbits to eat.

Mrs Hogget feeds Babe

And one day, for the first time…
Mrs Hogget Want to come in? Inside the house? Come on, then.

Mrs Hogget ushers Babe inside. Lights up on the farmhouse interior

Make yourself comfy, then.

Babe sits where Fly sat earlier

Want to watch a bit of telly?

She turns on the television, using the remote control. A familiar six o'clock news theme is heard, then audible but indistinguishable voices. Babe watches

Mrs Hogget starts mixing a pudding

Farmer Hogget enters downstage

Fly joins him, and then both enter the farmhouse interior

Farmer Hogget (*seeing Babe*) What's all this'n?
Babe (*unheard by the Hoggets*) Hi Mum!

Fly joins Babe, who squeezes up to accommodate her

Fly (*surprised*) Well, this is cosy.
Mrs Hogget He likes the telly, dear little chap.
Farmer Hogget Aah.
Mrs Hogget Just look at him. We should have brought him into the house long ago, no reason why not, is there now?
Farmer Hogget He might mess the carpet.
Mrs Hogget Never! He's no more likely to mess than he is to fly, he'll ask to go out when he wants to do his do's, just like a good clean dog would, got more brains that a dog he has, why 'twouldn't surprise me to hear he was rounding up them old sheep of yours, 'twouldn't honestly, though I suppose you think I'm daft.
Farmer Hogget No, you're not daft. (*He settles down with a piece of paper and a pen*)

Mrs Hogget is busy mixing her pudding

Fly (*to the audience*) Later that evening we watched a programme called "One Man and His Dog".

Babe Hey, Mum! Sheep and a sheep-dog!

Fly Trials. I used to do them.

Babe What's trials?

Fly A competition. To find the best sheep-dog. See the way that one's moving the sheep through the gaps and gateways.

Babe Did you ever win?

Fly No, dear.

Babe Did the boss mind?

Fly Well, I think he would have liked us to win.

They continue watching the television

Mrs Hogget Hogget, you're missing your programme.

Farmer Hogget Aah.

Mrs Hogget What bist you doing, anyways?

Farmer Hogget Writing.

Mrs Hogget takes the sheet of paper and reads it

Mrs Hogget (*surprised*) Grand Challenge Sheep-dog Trials. You's not thinking of entering the Grand Challenge?

Farmer Hogget Reckon as I might.

Mrs Hogget (*dismissively*) What a joke! Fly's far too old, be out of puff after five minutes! Grand Challenge! (*She laughs and hands back the entry form*)

Mrs Hogget exits

Music as Farmer Hogget deliberately and carefully fills in his form

Farmer Hogget "Name of Competitor", Farmer Hogget. "Name of Entry", P—I—G. (*He looks at Babe*) I reckon we has a chance, Pig…

The music swells as Babe and Fly look at Farmer Hogget, and the Lights change as the scene changes back to the farmyard

Fly comes forward to narrate

Fly (*to the audience*) We knew! We just knew what the boss was up to! The Grand Challenge! The first sheep-pig in the world to enter. But if he was to win, Babe needed some serious training!

Music introduces a training session, all choreographed—a set-piece montage full of movement and energetic fun. The music is jaunty exercise music, the sort of music that makes the audience want to clap in time (which indeed they may do)

First, Babe enters

Fly leads him in a kind of keep-fit class for pigs. Stretches, jumps, bends, press-ups perhaps if they don't look too human. An aerobics class for a pig...

Farmer Hogget enters

Perhaps the music allows him out of character, to act like a kind of ringmaster. He positions two straw bales and backs away as...

The Ducks enter

Encouraged by Fly, Babe "drives" the Ducks, making them circle and weave their way round Fly and through the straw bales. It is almost like a circus act

As the Ducks exit, Cockerel and Turkey enter and briefly get caught up in the swirl of activity

Then, as the music continues, Farmer Hogget blows his whistle and the scene changes to the field

The Sheep enter

With Farmer Hogget blowing his whistle, Babe works the Sheep. Farmer Hogget sets up obstacles and Babe successfully drives the Sheep through them

Eventually the training session ends with a flourish

The Sheep stay on stage, but Farmer Hogget, congratulating Babe, leads him off

Fly comes forward to narrate

(*To the audience*) Everything was going well. Babe was in great shape. But something was bothering me. Something that could spoil his chances. Something only the sheep might have the answer to. I'd never really spoken to sheep before—well, they're such stupid creatures—but I owed it to Babe to try. I swallowed my pride and went up to the field. (*She approaches the Sheep*)

The Sheep shuffle nervously

(*Ultra polite*) Good evening.
Sheep (*nervously*) Wolf! Wolf!
Fly (*nearly losing her cool and snapping*) No, no, I'm not a wolf. (*She recovers herself*) I'm Fly the sheep-dog, Babe's friend.
Sheep (*settling*) Aaaaah! Ba-a-a-a-abe!
Fly Yes. I wonder if you would be kind enough to help me. Well, help Babe, really.
Sheep Ba-a-a-a-abe!
Fly You see, tomorrow's his big day. He and the boss are taking part in the Grand Challenge Sheep-dog Trials. I know he's a pig, but he's as good as a dog, *you* know that. And that's the point. *You* know him. *You've* worked with him. But strange sheep, the sheep at the Trials, *won't* know him. How can he stop them running away at the sight of him? Please tell me. How can Babe gain their trust?

we

Pause, as the Sheep think

Sheep 1 Password.
Fly I beg your pardon?
Sheep 1 Password.
Sheep (*joining in*) Password. Pa-a-a-a-assword!
Sheep 1 What our Babe's got to do is larn what all of us larned when we was little lambs at our mothers' hocks.
Fly I see.
Sheep (*chanting*)   So then wherever we do go
                             To market or to fa-a-a-arm
                             If we do say the password
                             We'll never come to ha-a-a-arm!
Fly Please. Please will you tell me the password?

The Sheep consider. They turn inwards, forming a scrum. Fly looks on impatiently

Sheep 1 'Tis for Babe.
Sheep 'Tis for Babe! 'Tis for Ba-a-a-abe! (*They turn back to Fly. Mysteriously*) A-a-a-a-a-a-ah!

Then...

(*Intoning, as though in a trance*)   I may be ewe, I may be ram,

> I may be mutton, may be lamb,
> But on the hoof or on the hook,
> I 'bain't so stupid as I look.   Baa Ram Ewe

Fly Is that it? Please, again. (*She tries hard to remember*) I may be ewe, I may
be…

Sheep	… ra-a-a-am…
Fly	I may be mutton, may be…
Sheep	… la-a-a-amb…
Fly	But on the…
Sheep	… hoof…
Fly	… or on the…
Sheep	… hook…
All	I 'bain't so stupid as I look.

Baa Ram Ewe

The Sheep start to wander off

Fly Thank you.

Babe enters, listening

Thank you, dear, kind sheep!

Babe Mum, you're being polite!

Fly (*taken by surprise*) Maybe you've taught me something.

Babe Not as much as you've taught me.

Fly Listen, Babe, just in case the strange sheep tomorrow don't like you…

Babe Why shouldn't they like me?

Fly Listen, just in case they need calming down, *our* sheep have given you
some special words to say to them. You must learn them, Babe. They may
make all the difference. (*She starts the rhyme*) I may be … oh no, what was
it? (*To the audience*) Please, do you remember it? Help me teach it to Babe!
(*She leads the audience, but lets them help her with some of the words*)

> I may be ewe, I may be ram,
> I may be mutton, may be lamb,
> But on the hoof or on the hook,
> I 'baint so stupid as I look.   Baa Ram Ewe

(*To the audience*) Thank you!

Babe What does it mean, Mum?

Fly Meanings don't matter. Say it. (*To the audience*) Help him again, please!
(*She leads the audience joining in and prompting Babe*)

Babe (*with the audience*) I may be ewe, I may be ram,

> I may be mutton, may be lamb,
> But on the hoof or on the hook,
> I 'baint so stupid as I look.

Baa Ram Ewe

Fly Once more. Faster!

All
I may be ewe, I may be ram,
I may be mutton, may be lamb,
But on the hoof or on the hook,
I 'baint so stupid as I look. *Baa Ram Ewe*

Fly }
Babe } (*together*, *to the audience*) Thank you!

The Lighting fades. Babe sets off to meet the loose-box entering for the next scene. Fly steps forward to narrate

Fly (*to the audience*) That evening, the boss made the final preparations…

exit
12:00

Lights up on the loose-box, where Farmer Hogget energetically wields a scrubbing brush on Babe, occasionally dipping it in a bucket

Babe reacts but doesn't struggle

Mrs Hogget enters

Mrs Hogget Hogget! Supper's ready. And I've ironed you a nice clean shirt. (*She notices Babe*) Ha, what in the world bist doing polishing up the pig, all done up like a dog's dinner, or like a pig's dinner should I say, (*she sees Babe's bowl*) talking of which he's not eaten much tonight, 'as he? My, he's looking a treat, fit as a fiddlestick, anyone would think you was entering 'e tomorrow, not Fly, (*she laughs*) only he wouldn't be a sheep-dog, he'd be a sheep-pig, wouldn't 'e, (*she laughs*) whoever heard of such a daft thing? But you mustn't keep me talking, Hogget, supper's getting cold, (*she laughs on her way out*) a sheep-pig, don't make me laugh…

Mrs Hogget exits

Farmer Hogget looks up smiling and shaking his head. Little does she know…

He takes his pail and brush and starts to go, but suddenly he turns. Music as farmer and pig gaze into each other's eyes, just as they did at the guess-my-weight stall. An equally significant moment as they contemplate tomorrow's competition

Then…

Farmer Hogget Night, Pig.

Farmer Hogget leaves

Babe, alone, recites the password, pausing to remember certain words. Hopefully the audience prompts him

Babe I may be ewe, you may be me ... no, no...
I may be ewe, I may be ... ram,
I may be mutton, may be ham ... no, no ... lamb,
But on the ... hoof or on the ... hook,
I 'baint so stupid as I look.
(Baa~ from Ewe)

Fly enters 12:00

Fly All right, dear?
Babe Yes, Mum.
Fly Ready for your big day?
Babe Yes, Mum.
Fly Nervous?
Babe Yes, Mum.
Fly You'll be great.
Babe (*after a pause*) Yes, Mum.
Fly Sleep well, Babe. (*She starts to go*)
Babe (*suddenly*) Mum?
Fly Yes?
Babe (*softly*) I love you.
Fly I love you too.

Fly exits 12:00

Babe settles to sleep

A distant rumble of thunder disturbs him. He nervously closes his eyes

The Lighting begins to change. We hear an echoing laugh, distracted and scary. And strange, eerie music

Babe's nightmare begins

Nightmarish animals come to haunt him, perhaps wearing large distorted heads. Cockerel, Worrier-dog, Sheep, Ducks, Turkey, Cat

In a slow choreographed sequence they enter one by one, circling Babe, who "wakes" and joins the nightmare animals, nervously seeing each one and trying to escape from the circle

11:00

Meanwhile the Lighting echoes the nightmarish feel. Perhaps a strobe?

The sound incorporates distorted laughter with voices reminding Babe of moments in the play when he felt fear or danger. Occasional snatches of his own squealing, plus thunder, Ma's cough, the Sheep's bleating lament and Farmer Hogget's whistle

Cockerel Cock-a-doodle-poooooo!
Puppy It's ugly! It's horrible!
Fly Pigs are stupid.
Babe I want my mum.
Puppy He'll wet the bed!
Turkey I gobble and I peck.
Babe It's no good, Mum. I tell them what to do, but they won't listen!
Sheep Wolf! Wolf! Ba-a-a-a-a-a-a!
Rustler Get him! Get him!
Babe Oh Ma, oh Ma, oh Ma...
Farmer Hogget Come by, Pig!
Babe They won't listen!
Mrs Hogget A sheep-pig? Whoever heard of such a daft thing?
Farmer Hogget Come by, Pig!
Babe They won't listen!
Farmer Hogget Come by, Pig!
Babe They won't listen! They won't listen! They won't listen!

By the time the nightmare reaches its climax, Babe is alone as the sounds of laughter build and reverberate in his head. As the Lighting focuses on him, the scene changes, so that at the very peak of the nightmare, suddenly it stops

The Lights come up and we are back at the Grand Challenge Sheep-dog Trials   at 7:00

Babe is standing next to Farmer Hogget, as he was before Fly introduced the play-within-a-play. The Sheep huddle upstage

The laughter of the crowd continues as the TV Commentator returns and picks up his commentary

TV Commentator Oh, good heavens! I don't believe it! It *is* a pig! Well, this is ridiculous. Farmer Hogget can't be serious. I think he *is* serious. He'll be disqualified, surely. He can't enter a pig! Or maybe he can! Unprecedented scenes here as the officials check the rule book.

Two harassed officials enter, studying a rule book, shaking their heads in disbelief

The action freezes and the laughter cuts out as the Lights come up on the farmhouse interior, which either enters now or was set as the nightmare ended. (NB: In the original production, the farmhouse would have taken up too much space, so just a chair was used, recognisable from the interior scene)

Mrs Hogget enters. She turns on the television, using the remote control

Mrs Hogget (*talking to herself*) So busy doing me chores, nearly forgot to turn the telly on, don't want to miss nothing, though why he's entered's a mystery, the depths of what I cannot fathom. Don't stand a chance with dear old Fly, past it she be...

The picture comes up

...oh well, I never, there be Hogget, looking 'andsome though I says it meself, so where's Fly, then, come on cameraman, move your camera, that's the way... (*A sudden gasp as she sees Babe. She points to the screen in amazement. For the first time in her life she is lost for words. She freezes, eyes riveted to the television screen*)

The showground action unfreezes

The two officials close the book, nodding as they exit

TV Commentator Well, it looks as if ... yes, there seems to be nothing in the rule book that says only sheep-dogs can compete. So it looks as though the judges can't stop Farmer Hogget running his, er, sheep-pig I suppose we'll have to call it (*he laughs*). But it really is making a mockery of the Grand Challenge. One look at a pig and the sheep will disappear into the next county! Still, we may as well end the afternoon with a good laugh. And the weather's cheering up too! Here we go, then. Farmer Hogget and Pig!

Farmer Hogget turns upstage to face the Sheep. He blows his whistle

Farmer Hogget Come by, Pig.

A musical pulse begins as Babe sets off. He approaches the Sheep

Babe Good afternoon.

The Sheep shuffle restlessly

Sheep Wolf! Wolf! Baaaa!

Babe No, I'm not a wolf, I…

The Sheep start turning away

Please.

Fly suddenly appears downstage

Fly (*calling*) Password! Give the password!
Babe (*confused*) Er … yes… You may be I … no!
Fly (*to the audience*) Please, everybody, help Babe! Say it with me! (*She leads the audience*)

> I may be ewe, I may be ram,
> I may be mutton, may be lamb,
> But on the hoof or on the hook,
> I 'bain't so stupid as I look. Baa Ram Ewe

Thank you.
Babe (*slowly but very deliberately to the Sheep*)

> I may be ewe, I may be ram,
> I may be mutton, may be lamb,
> But on the hoof or on the hook,
> I bain't so stupid as I look.

Baa Ram Ewe

The musical pulse continues as the Sheep slowly turn back to Babe

Sheep 1 The pa-a-a-a-assword!
Sheep He knows the pa-a-a-a-assword!

They listen

Babe Please, would you let me work with you?
Sheep 1 What lovely ma-a-a-a-anners!
Sheep What d'you want us to do, young ma-a-a-a-aster?

The Sheep huddle round Babe, who mimes talking to them

TV Commentator Well, a bit of a hiatus here. But in fairness the sheep haven't run away. Maybe the pig's explaining the course to them. (*He laughs*)
Babe (*stepping back*) Thank you so much. Steady pace. Stick together. Off we go!

Music as the Sheep, controlled by Babe, step with military precision, almost like a dance, perfectly in time with the music. The effect should be totally unlike anything we have seen the Sheep do up to now

They calmly and efficiently follow the route we saw earlier. Down through the Fetch Gates, round Farmer Hogget, through the Drive Away Gates, across to the Cross Drive Gates and through, then into the Shedding ring, where they stop perfectly

TV Commentator Amazing. He hasn't put a foot wrong. No wonder the crowd has gone silent. Lovely pace, bang through the middle of the gates. Perfect. And Farmer Hogget hasn't said a word! But now comes the real test. Believe me, there is no possibility of a pig shedding sheep. If he does that I'll eat my hat.

Again, a musical pulse

Farmer Hogget raises his crook and gives the ground a sharp tap

Babe approaches the Sheep

Babe Beautifully done. I'm so grateful to you. Now, if the four ladies with the nice red collars would kindly walk out of the ring…

The four collared Sheep calmly separate themselves from the others

Farmer Hogget walks to the pen

Thank you ladies. Now, everybody, this way please.

Babe leads the Sheep towards the pen. They all enter. The Lighting suggests the sun has come out. Suddenly we hear wild cheering and applause

Farmer Hogget leads Babe c, where they acknowledge the applause

TV Commentator (*over the continuing applause*) He did it! He did it! That was fantastic! In thirty years I've never seen such a display. I'm eating my hat. Truly, I'm eating my hat! That was a perfect round, surely?

The officials run on, holding up cards showing a one and two noughts

It was! It was! A perfect round! The pig scored a maximum unheard of hundred points!

In the farmhouse interior, Mrs Hogget unfreezes and applauds wildly

Fly joins Farmer Hogget and greets Babe

The applause and cheering continue as the officials bring in a huge Challenge cup. They present it to Farmer Hogget

And the Grand Challenge Cup goes to Farmer Hogget and Pig, the one and only *sheep-pig*!

The TV Commentator rushes up to Farmer Hogget and sticks a microphone under his face. The applause tails off

Farmer Hogget, many congratulations, and to Pig, of course. A remarkable achievement. Please, for all our viewers, what have you got to say?

A long pause

Farmer Hogget smiles. He looks down at Babe

Farmer Hogget That'll do.

Black-out

After a quick CURTAIN *call, the whole cast, encouraging the audience to join in clapping and shouting, perform a joyful reprise of the dance we saw earlier, celebrating Babe's victory over the Rustlers. All triumphantly and exuberantly shout "Babe" at the end of each phrase. If appropriate, the cast could dance out through the auditorium, leaving Babe and Fly to wave final goodbyes*

FURNITURE AND PROPERTY LIST

Further dressing may be added at the director's discretion

ACT I

On stage: Banner: "Grand Challenge Sheep-dog Trials"
           Obstacles (fences or straw bales) to double as fairground stalls

Off stage: Umbrella, microphone (**TV Commentator**)
           2 cards showing "8" and "5" (**Official**)

Personal: **Shepherd:** whistle, crook
           Farmer Hogget: whistle, crook

During the scene change on page 3

Strike: Banner

Re-set: Fences or straw bales as fairground stalls

Off stage: Clipboard (**Vicar**)
           Basket of goodies covered with a cloth (**Farmer Hogget**)
           Phone (**Mrs Hogget**)

Personal: **Farmer Hogget:** mobile phone, coin
           Weight Guesser 2: money

During the scene change on page 6

Strike: Fairground stalls

Re-set: Straw bales as stable loose-box

Off stage: Water-bowl (**Farmer Hogget**)

During the scene change on page 10

Strike: Straw bales as stable loose-box

Off stage: Bowl of slops (**Mrs Hogget**)
             Trough of dog food (**Farmer Hogget**)
             2 straw bales (**Farmer Hogget**)

Personal: **New Owner 1:** money
             New Owner 2: money
             New Owner 3: money

During the scene change on page 15

Re-set: Straw bales as stable loose-box

During the scene change on page 16

Strike: Straw bales as stable loose-box

Set: Farmhouse interior
             Television
             Remote control
             Dough
             Phone

During the scene change on page 17

Set: Sheep pen
             Rear of lorry with tailgate

Personal: **Rustlers:** large sticks, torches

During the scene change on page 19

Strike: Lorry
             Sheep pen

Off stage: Double-barrelled shotgun (**Farmer Hogget**)

Personal: **Farmer Hogget:** whistle, crook

ACT II

Off stage: Double-barrelled shotgun containing cartridges (**Farmer Hogget**)
Phone (**Mrs Hogget**)

Personal: **Farmer Hogget:** mobile phone

During the scene change on page 26

Off stage: Feed (**Mrs Hogget**)

During the scene change on page 27

Set: Farmhouse interior
Television
Remote control
Phone
Pudding
Piece of paper, pen

During the scene change on page 28

Off stage: 2 straw bales (**Farmer Hogget**)

Personal: **Farmer Hogget:** whistle

During the scene change on page 29

Strike: Straw bales

During the scene change on page 32

Set: Straw bales as loose-box
Scrubbing brush
Bucket
Babe's bowl

During the scene change on page 33

Strike: Straw bales as loose-box
Babe's bowl

During the scene change on page 34

Set: Banner: "Grand Challenge Sheep-dog Trials"
              Obstacles (fences or straw bales)
              Sheep pen

Off stage: Umbrella, microphone (**TV Commentator**)
              Rule book (**Officials**)

During the scene change on page 35

Set: Farmhouse interior
              Television
              Remote control

Off stage: 3 cards showing "1", "0", and "0" (**Officials**)
              Huge Challenge cup (**Officials**)

Personal: **Farmer Hogget:** whistle, crook

LIGHTING PLOT

Property fittings required: nil
Various interior and exterior settings

ACT I

Cue 11   **Babe**: "Night, Mum."   (Page 9)
            Change lighting slowly for night to dawn transition

Cue 12   **Fly** enters   (Page 13)
            Fade lights down; spot on **Fly**

Cue 13   Four **Ducks** enter   (Page 14)
            Bring up lighting

Cue 14   Clap of thunder, then rain   (Page 15)
            Fade lights down

Cue 15   **Farmer Hogget** exits   (Page 15)
            Fade up lighting

Cue 16   **Ma** settles to sleep   (Page 16)
            Fade lighting

Cue 17   **Fly** crosses to the farmhouse   (Page 16)
            Spot on **Farmer Hogget** *and* **Mrs Hogget**,
                television effect

Cue 18   **Mrs Hogget** attacks the dough   (Page 17)
            Fade lights on the farmhouse, bring up half light on field

Cue 19   Screech of brakes   (Page 18)
            Lorry silhouette and tail lights effect (optional)

Cue 20   **Rustlers** enter with torches   (Page 18)
            Snap on back-up lighting

Cue 21   **Babe**'s squeal echoes nightmarishly   (Page 19)
            Fade lighting for scene change, then bring up
                on farmhouse

Cue 22   Police car siren blares   (Page 20)
            Black-out; police car lamp effect

Cue 23   Police siren fades   (Page 20)
            Lights up on the farmyard

Cue 24   Menacing music   (Page 23)
            Fade lights down

Cue 25	**Farmer Hogget** aims shotgun at **Babe**	(Page 24)
	Black-out	

ACT II

To open:	Low general lighting	
Cue 26	**Mrs Hogget** enters	(Page 25)
	Spot on **Mrs Hogget**	
Cue 27	**Mrs Hogget** exits	(Page 25)
	Cut spot on **Mrs Hogget**	
Cue 28	The procession exits	(Page 26)
	Fade lights slowly to black-out	
Cue 29	**Mrs Hogget** ushers **Babe** in the farmhouse	(Page 27)
	Lights up on farmhouse interior	
Cue 30	**Mrs Hogget** turns on the television	(Page 27)
	Television effect	
Cue 31	**Babe** and **Fly** look at **Farmer Hogget**	(Page 28)
	Crossfade to farmyard	
Cue 32	**Fly** and **Babe**: "Thank you!"	(Page 32)
	Fade lights	
Cue 33	**Fly**: "…made the final preparations…"	(Page 32)
	Lights up on the loose-box	
Cue 34	**Babe** nervously closes his eyes	(Page 33)
	Slowly bring up nightmarish lighting; strobe (optional)	
Cue 35	Babe is alone at nightmare climax	(Page 34)
	Cut nightmare lighting, bring up spot on Babe,	
	then bring up lighting on trials scene	
Cue 36	The action freezes	(Page 35)
	Bring up lighting on farmhouse interior	
Cue 37	**Mrs Hogget**: "…past it she be…"	(Page 35)
	Television effect	

Cue 38   **Sheep** enter pen   (Page 37)
            Bring up sunny lighting

Cue 39   **Farmer Hogget**: "That'll do."   (Page 38)
            Black-out

EFFECTS PLOT

See note on page vi regarding optional incidental music

ACT I

Cue 12	**Farmer Hogget**: "What noise?" *Another squeal, longer and louder*	(Page 4)
Cue 13	**Weight-Guesser 2** lifts the pig *More squealing*	(Page 5)
Cue 14	**Weight-Guesser 2** puts the pig down *Cut squealing*	(Page 5)
Cue 15	**Farmer Hogget** gives the **Vicar** a coin *Music*	(Page 5)
Cue 16	**Farmer Hogget** and **Babe** look at each other *Change music to heighten significance, continuing*	(Page 6)
Cue 17	**Farmer Hogget** and **Babe** break their freeze *Change music; cut when ready*	(Page 6)
Cue 18	**Babe** cuddles up to **Fly** *Music; cut when ready*	(Page 8)
Cue 19	**Farmer Hogget** and **Mrs Hogget** exit *Music; cut when ready*	(Page 9)
Cue 20	**Babe**: "Night, Mum." *Music to suggest night to dawn transition*	(Page 9)
Cue 21	**Fly, Puppies** and **Babe** stir and stretch *Music as appropriate*	(Page 9)
Cue 22	**Fly** leads **Puppies** and **Babe** round the farmyard *Music as appropriate*	(Page 10)
Cue 23	**Mrs Hogget** enters *Music as appropriate*	(Page 11)
Cue 24	**Fly** joins **Babe** and **Puppies** *Music as appropriate, continuing*	(Page 13)
Cue 25	Four **Ducks** enter *Change music as appropriate*	(Page 14)
Cue 26	**Babe** exits *Clap of thunder, then rain, continuing softly*	(Page 15)

Cue 27	**Babe** slips away *Clap of thunder*	(Page 16)
Cue 28	**Farmer Hogget** and **Mrs Hogget** watch television *Sport programme on television; cut when ready*	(Page 16)
Cue 29	Lighting fades on farmhouse *Music, continuing*	(Page 17)
Cue 30	**Ma**: "Very kind, I'm sure, but…" *Loud, menacing rumble of a lorry approaching,* *engine continues running*	(Page 17)
Cue 31	**Ma**: "Hush!" *Screech of brakes, then loud echoing noises of doors* *opening and slamming, music underscoring tension*	(Page 18)
Cue 32	Two **Rustlers** wind down the tailboard of the lorry *Loud, echoing chain-rattling sounds, clunking thud as* *tailboard hits ground*	(Page 18)
Cue 33	Fight with **Rustlers** ends *Musical chord of triumph, then **Babe**'s piercing squeal* *of warning echoes nightmarishly during scene change*	(Page 19)
Cue 34	**Farmer Hogget** dials 999 *Police car siren blares out, taking over from the* *squealing; fade when ready*	(Page 19)
Cue 35	**Babe** enters *Music as appropriate*	(Page 20)
Cue 36	**Babe**, **Fly** and **Farmer Hogget** set off to the field *Music as appropriate*	(Page 20)
Cue 37	**Sheep**: "We want Ba-a-a-a-be!" *Music for tension, strange, almost magical, similar* *to Cue 16*	(Page 21)
Cue 38	**Fly** exits *Menacing music*	(Page 23)

ACT II